What I learned about Depression & Anxiety

Written and Illustrated by
Matt Frey

Copyright © 2020 Matt Frey
All rights reserved.

This book or any portion thereof may not be reproduced or used in any manner whatsoever without the express written permission of the publisher except for the use of brief quotations in a book review.

Printed in the United States of America

First Printing, 2020

ISBN 978-1-63337-373-0

For business inquiries contact
spaztastic.comic@gmail.com

PLEASE READ!

I am not a licensed therapist or counselor, nor is this book intended to diagnose or treat depression or anxiety. This is not a substitute for actual medical counsel.

The intention of this book is to use anecdotal experience to help spread awareness of these conditions to those that may suffer unknowingly or to inform those that don't suffer but wish to understand a modicum of how it feels. Hopefully this book helps encourage people to find a path to mental wellness and invest in their well being.

Thanks for reading!
-Matt Frey

This was the first piece I drew that led me to make this entire series. It was one of those nights where I just laid in my bed, not able to sleep, and I was feeling the worst I had ever felt. By some miracle I was able to force myself to get up and start drawing.

It originally only had "Sometimes it's hard to keep fighting." Hours later when I had come out of my depressive low, the second part was added. As such, this became the beginning of everything. This was my banner that I marched under, to keep fighting, to start to get better.

This entry is a little "off topic" I suppose. More so this one came about after thinking over how much of our own self worth we tie into how we look in the mirror. These thoughts can be related a little into how unlovable or invisible we can feel if we don't have the traits we want. This can absolutely feed into depression. I'm guilty of thinking these thoughts; as are a lot of the people who are reading this right now.

I remember looking into the mirror before drawing this page out. At first there were the thoughts of "Oh god, you're so fat. How did you get like this?" and "Who could want you like this?" Pushing a little beyond those negative thought I began to say things like, "This isn't all of who you are, this reflection isn't representative of your worth."

Anxiety is another key player in mental health. It seems that a lot of the time it comes hand in hand with depression. I personally didn't start feeling the effects of anxiety until I had already started showing symptons of being depressed.

In a lot of situations anxiety can act as a little voice in the back of your head, warning you about impending dangers. The point where this becomes a problem is when we start seeing social events, new people, new places and different situations as a perceived danger. Our little anxiety alarm goes off and tries to tell us that something is wrong. In this instance it can tell us that isolating ourselves is the safest thing to do.

In this illustration we see anxiety ringing the alarm about new people. Regardless of their actual intentions, we can get the feeling that they are potentially dangerous or unsafe. You can argue that this is a product of the times or that this is situationally helpful. Again, the problem comes in that it's not generally pick and choose. People that suffer from anxiety sometimes live day to day with this guard up.

Imagine your friends inviting you to go to a new restauraunt and you get this sudden panic, a sinking feeling in your stomach, or your heart rate increasing. All that just from the thought of being in a new place, with new people. From there you can placate your anxiety to stay home, or risk pushing the boundaries of your anxiety and go.

Anxiety can make us feel like...

...we are surrounded by Monsters

Regardless of what you suffer from, seeking out a therapist/counselor can make all the difference in your mental health. There are some situations that trying to overcome them with sheer willpower isn't the best option available. I got a taste of that personally. Laying in my dark room just trying to will myself past what I was feeling. In my case, not only did that not help, it made me feel worse. There was a built up resentment that I couldn't just climb out of it.

There is also a harmful myth that only "broken" people go to therapy. Not only is this flat out not true, it toxifies the idea of going to seek out help. It can be an amazing experience and hopefully it can sometimes prevent a worse situation from starting. They can help give you a toolbox of useful mechanisms for self analysis and coping devices.

This thought may be a bit more controversial than others represented in this book. I personally think that there are lifestyles that we can adopt that can perceivably help us through our roughest times. For some people, myself included, there is the option of getting medications prescribed to help alleviate the symptoms of depression. Some people can turn to meditation to center themselves, possibly in conjunction with therapy. There are also those that can find comfort in religion. Lastly, though some would disagree, there are people that find help through using marijuana to tame some of the symptoms of depression. You don't have to just use one thing, nor are you limited to what I've listed. What I would find intolerable is judging or forsaking another persons methodology unless it is actually hurting themselves or others.

Too many times I have found myself alone, drowning in my most depressive thoughts. Without help from friends, family, therapists, or doctors we can find ourselves just steeped in our own perception. Some people have a natural instinct to withdraw into themselves when we feel the waves of depression lap at our feet. If we create a bubble and isolate ourselves in it, those waters that we are struggling with have nowhere to go except to fill up the space around us. That is why it is important to develop tools to help us and build a support network to pull us back to the safety of the shore.

This is another huge, dangerous obstacle people struggling with their mental health are faced with. Another reason why building the right support network is so incredibly important. People that don't understand what it's like to struggle with these issues can, regardless of their intention, detract from or disregard the truth of a persons situation. Some of these people are earnestly trying to help in the ways that they know how, while a toxic variety of people will seek to dismantle and belittle the struggle of people who are suffering. It is up to you to figure out what helps you.

Probably one of the most common and talked about symptoms of depression is the loss of interest in things that you love doing. In most cases for myself I couldn't bring myself to pick up a pencil, play an instrument, read, or even play video games. Getting out of bed was challenging enough, let alone trying to bring myself to do something productive. It got to the point where I started missing too much class and jeopardized my academic career.

That leads into a slightly less talked about symptom that is, from my experience, also common amongst depressed people. That would be the lack of self care such as: personal hygene, organization, cleaning, and other tasks necessary to maintain ones own household.

Depression can make you...

...lose interest in what you love.

A huge mistake I made with my own personal mental health was concluding that I must be fine since I didn't feel depressed in that moment. I thought that it had been conquered or not very severe since it wore off. Depression isn't always a feeling you get every second of every day. It can come in waves, start in on a moments notice. Trying to only seek help when you are in the midst of it is akin to only breathing when you feel the wind.

Just because you don't feel it every day doesn't mean you're not depressed.

Another aspect of depression that people can't always comprehend is that, even if things are fine situationally, you can still become depressed. You could have everything in the world to look forward to and can still fall into a hole. It can feel like things will never get better and that this hole you're in is the best it will ever be. Objectively it is not true but trying to argue logic to yourself in a depressed state is often a futile uphill task. This is another situation where having a lifestyle, therapy, or medication that can help equip you to climb out or miss the hole are so vital. People that don't have these issues may find themselves frustrated with trying to "convince" someone to leave their pit of depression. It's very important to try understanding the perspective of who they are trying to help.

For people that elect or need to pursue medication to help with their depression, it can be very frustrating finding the right fit for you. It can take some trial and error to find the right balance of side effects, dosage, and benefit of each medicine. I know people that have sworn off getting prescriptions due to the bad experiences they have had. The fact is that there are so many different medications out there that it is impossible for a doctor to know the exact right one to begin with. With that in mind we have to find the patience to bear with it. Our mental wellness is well worth it.

You don't always get it right at first

but don't get discouraged.

Depression has a way of constantly being a voice inside your head. I personally struggle with trying to shake out the negative thoughts that are fed directly into my mind. It piles on until it's a reverberated screaming that becomes harder to mute as it layers onto itself. What that negative voice starts with could be as simple as "Your friends have more fun when you're not around." Once it gets a foothold it can leak into other things.

This is probably one of the hardest parts for me to describe to people that are not afflicted with depression. People have a hard time realizing how rooted and difficult it is to defend against the lies being broadcast into your conscious. It doesn't have to be as grim as it sounds if you take the right precautions. Therapists can introduce you to helpful techniques and affirmations to prevent it with practice.

An important thing to remember as you are trying to decide whether or not to seek diagnosis or treatment is that depression is not just one certain type symptoms. Depression does not always manifest in people the same way. We use the generic lack of interest, sense of dread, and a few other common indicators. However there are a many more ways that it can show up in yourself or loved ones. I know that I personally deal with sudden mood shifts, I'm quick to become angry or frustrated and quickly disconnect emotionally.

So with all of the variations in symptoms it may feel like it's impossible to tell if you have depression, but that is where seeking a therapist or even just talking to a doctor can help significantly. Also, with the variations in symptoms, the treatment won't always be the same. This is critical in deciding to get treated, especially if you or someone you know had a bad experience.

Depression doesn't look the same on everyone...

...nor is it treated the same

Seeking treatment may sound like you are going in to be cured of your depression, but it's not exactly that simple. Depression can be a long, long battle. Some people may get frustrated that they still have times where they are overwhelmed in their depression despite being in a care plan. That's why I like to think that winning more rounds opposing depression is definitely a sign of getting better. It means that through the plans you are using, you are mastering the tools and the medicine, or lifestyle changes, that will help you fight back even better. It's very important to see these battles, the wins and losses, through a positive perspective.

Sometimes getting better is just winning more battles than you lose.

Even though it's talked about earlier in this book, I think it's important to emphasize the fact that mental wellness has many paths to achieve the same results. The path isn't even a singular one, sometimes it's best to straddle a few different avenues in conjuction. In this drawing, as well as earlier, it shows just a few such ways. Listed are : Medical Wellness, Therapy, and Life Improvements. What I mean in terms of Medical Wellness would be things like medications, as well as physical health. Our mental health can be associated and affected by our bodies. Therapy is pretty straight forward but worth mentioning that it's not only meant for "broken" people and is often just a good idea. Life Improvement is a little bit of a grey area. For me, it meant putting time and effort into my dreams. For other people it can be something else like moving, changing jobs or making more time for yourself.

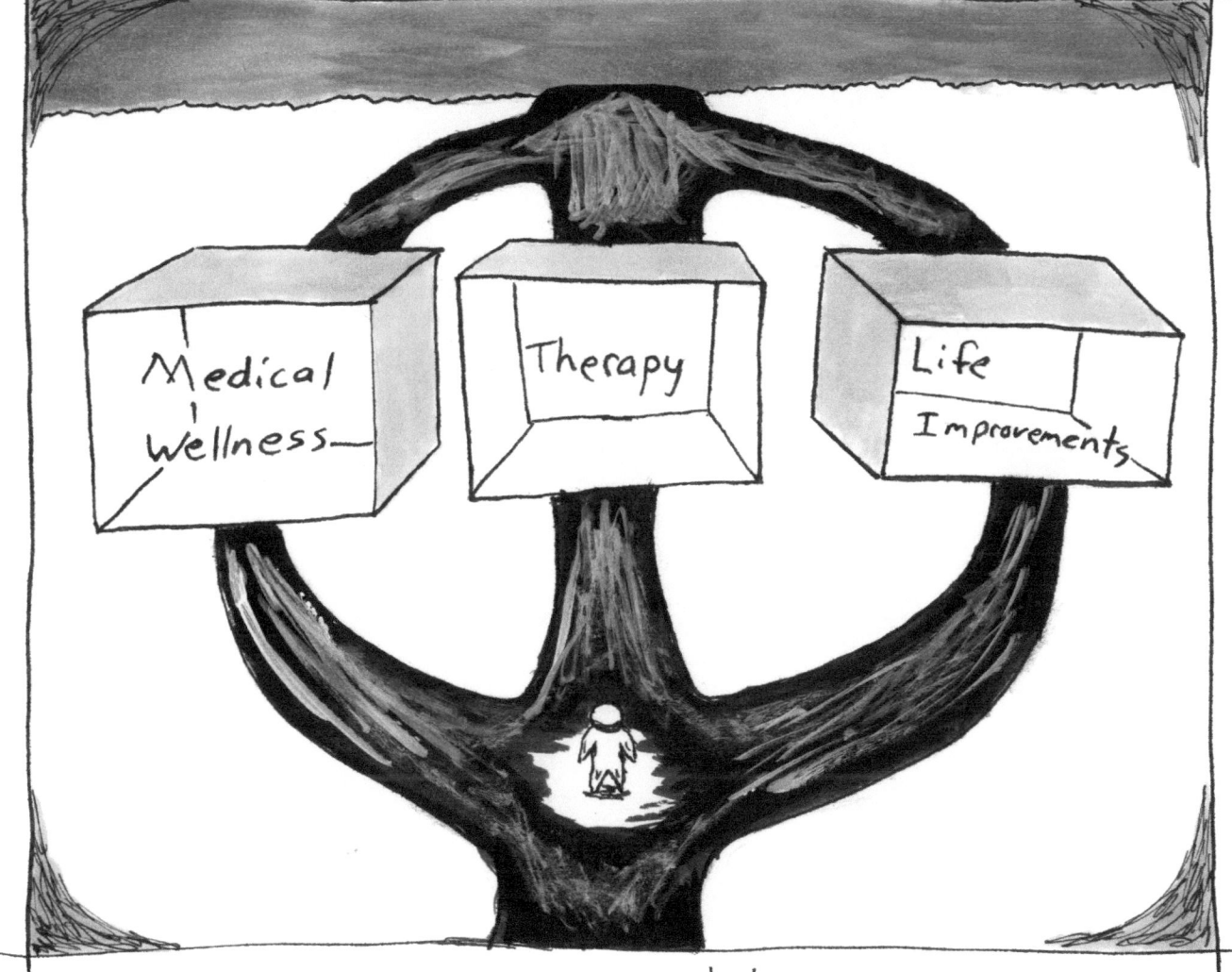

Starting down the path to mental wellness is amazing and it can help you feel better than you probably thought you could again, however, it's so very important to remind people on their way that it is a continual effort. For a lot of us it isn't as easy as completing a set of steps and graduating from depression or anxiety. This isn't something to discourage people from embarking on the voyage, it is to guard against discouragement. If you happen to suffer a few losses, it is much easier to get disheartened if you think it isn't working.

Mental Health Wellness...

...is a continual Journey.

This entry ties well into the previous one. Wondering if what you're doing is even helping, how you'll be able to tell, or even what it'll feel like to not feel the way you are right now. I had to ask myself what some of the happiest times of my life were and try to remember how I felt; would the treatment help me feel that way again? I can say from personal experience that, at the very least, I don't feel like I'm being emotionally attacked from all directions. What these questions are for other people fighting with it, or what their answers will be, I can't say for sure. These answers will have to come from you because my experience, like we talked about before, is very different from what you're going through.

This one will be a little difficult to talk through as well but I think it can tie in very well to some things we discussed earlier. To some people, they may not recognize a "trigger" for their depression or anxiety. What I mean when I say "trigger" is an event, situation or setting that flares up depression or anxiety. To this day, I don't fully understand what mine is but I feel like I'm getting there. What these are for you, or people you know suffering from one of these conditions, are for you to discover. Some people already know what does it for them and that will give you a jumping off point for dealing with it through therapy, meditation or whatever helps you. If you discover what starts these feeling for you, it may help you understand how to fight it.

This fits into "lifestyle improvements" but surrounding yourself with the right people can help dramatically when you're dealing with depression or anxiety. Having a support system of people that either understand what it's like to feel the way you feel or at least are willing to sympathize with it makes all the difference. People that are dismissive of your anxiety and pushy with your depression are not the people that will help you with your path of mental wellness. This doesn't always mean that they are bad people or bad friends, but perhaps just not fully informed on what you're dealing with.

You should find the right...

...people to surround yourself with.

The difficult thing about how some people experience depression is that it can come on very quickly, before we even realize that it's there. If we are not prepared then it can make us spiral very quickly. In therapy they teach methods of interrupting the cycle before it can take you down. The difference between the beginning of the spiral to the bottom is the difference between "My friends have more fun when I'm not there" and "Everyone is better off without me." This is why it's important to learn ways to keep your thoughts from falling down this dark rabbit hole. What I've learned from my personal struggle is that medication can help keep your thoughts from hitting the bottom.

This panel feels pretty self explanatory but it can't be stated how much of a help therapy can be with or without depression, anxiety, or any other condition. I know that there are some negative stereotypes we put on the idea of counseling but I can personally assure you that not every experience is like the portrayal that they show on TV shows. You will get some questions like, "And how does that make you feel?" If you take the opportunity to answer honestly and push past the feeling of being "embarassingly vulnerable" those questions can become a powerful introspective.

I believe that sometimes we can spend too much time in our respective depression pits that it feels like those thoughts and feeling are just normal. It can become hard to differentiate how depression changes your thoughts versus how your thoughts and feelings operate when we are outside of depressive episodes. For me, I have to remind myself that when I start to have darker thoughts that I am in fact still suffering from depression and that these thoughts are passing. It's a little difficult to put into words but suffice to say that it's worth checking yourself and give yourself a reminder that these are feelings are coming from a place outside of your healthy mindset.

Although we didn't spend a lot of time talking about anxiety, it's equally a painful experience to go through. Anxiety has far too many causes to begin to make generalizations of how to describe it, but one thing is for sure; it makes most days a challenge. Speaking from my own experience, anxiety feels a little bit like my mind very suddenly turns on my flight or fight response. Unfortunately, it can cause quite a few other feelings for people that have to deal with it. People can succumb to panic attacks, or something of the like, if pushed too hard into a situation that already fills them with anxiety. Just like depression, it can come on quite suddenly and make it hard to navigate everday tasks.

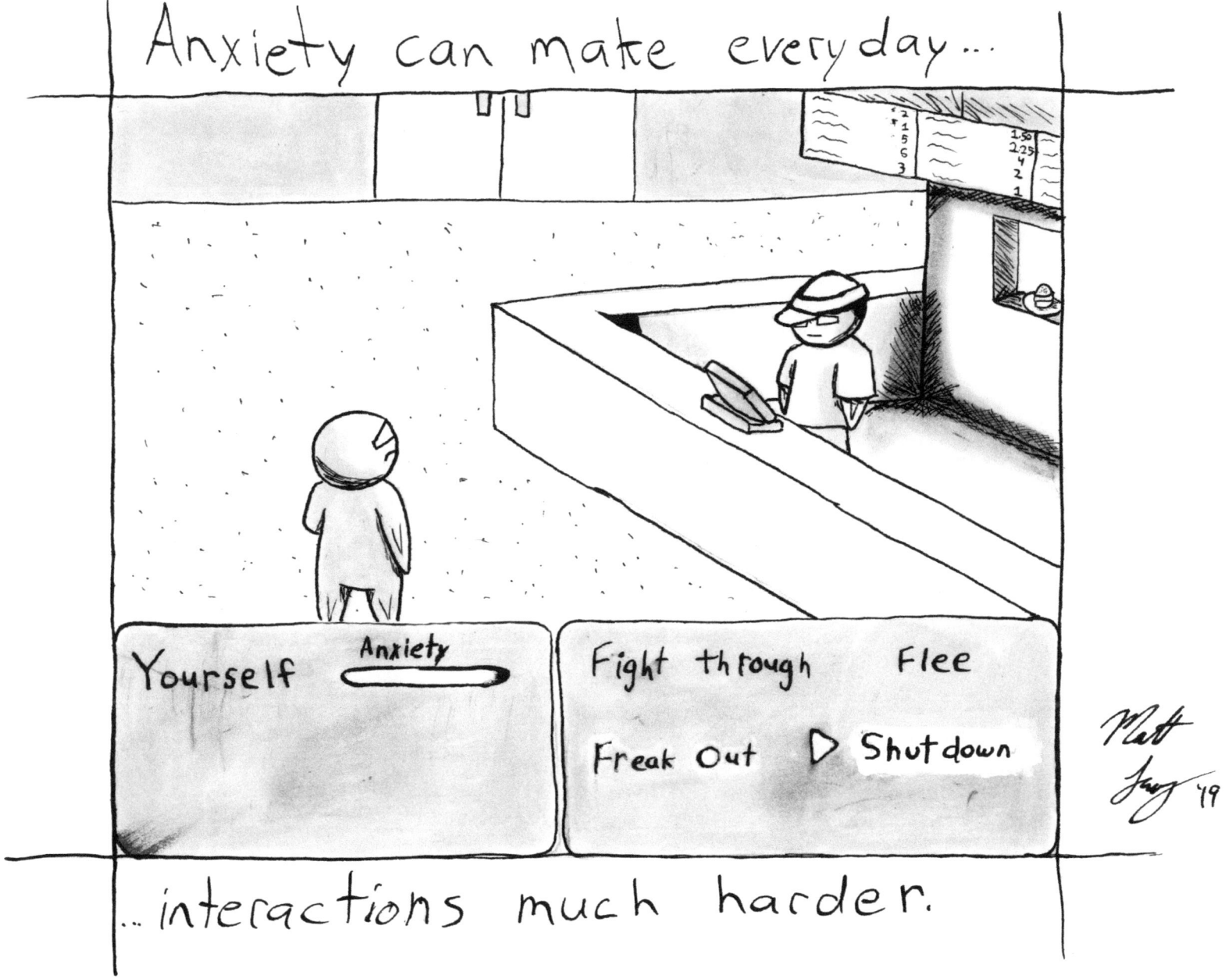

A lot of ads, friends, doctors, and advocates will tell you to pick up the phone if you are starting to feel depressed, but it's worth taking a second to acknowledge how hard that can be. It seems soo simple and incredibly easy to just grab your phone to text or call someone. What people that don't suffer with depression can find hard to understand is that, with depression whispering it's lies in your head, a simple task becomes a hard battle. What I'd like you to know is that no matter how hard it seems, or what kind of isolationist thoughts your mind lets leak in, you are strong enough to pick up the phone and the people that said you can talk to them absolutely want to hear from you.

Throughout this whole book, I've advocated receiving treatment and creating care plans for yourself, but I've taken great care to let you know that there is no cure all. There is not one simple answer to treating everything. This page is a cautionary tale for people that may be tempted to try cure alls and quick fixes instead of putting the work into making yourself better. It's easy to get your hopes up and defer to ad campaigns offering to make you feel better, but these people are just trying to sell buzzword products to generations of people that are tired of feeling the way they do. I can't tell you what's right or wrong, or even what will work best for you, but I can assure you that it's not so simple that a pill or ointment will permanently fix everything.

www.ingramcontent.com/pod-product-compliance
Lightning Source LLC
Chambersburg PA
CBHW041949080426

42734CB00004B/73